MARTIN'S DREAM

For Yohannes and his dream of books
in the hands of Ethiopian children —J. K.

To Michael and Amanda
—A. J.-B.

ALADDIN PAPERBACKS
An imprint of Simon & Schuster Children's Publishing Division
1230 Avenue of the Americas, New York, NY 10020
Text copyright © 2008 by Jane Kurtz
Illustrations copyright © 2008 by Amy June Bates
All rights reserved, including the right of reproduction in whole or in part in any form.
ALADDIN PAPERBACKS, READY-TO-READ, and related logo are registered
trademarks of Simon & Schuster, Inc.
Designed by Lisa Vega
The text of this book was set in 24pt Century Oldstyle BT.
Manufactured in the United States of America
First Aladdin Paperbacks edition November 2008
2 4 6 8 10 9 7 5 3
Library of Congress Cataloging-in-Publication Data
Kurtz, Jane.
Martin's dream / by Jane Kurtz ; illustrated by Amy June Bates.
— 1st Aladdin Paperbacks ed.
p. cm. — (Ready-to-read)
1. King, Martin Luther, Jr., 1929–1968—Juvenile literature.
2. King, Martin Luther, Jr., 1929–1968. I have a dream—Juvenile literature.
3. African Americans—Civil rights—History—20th century—Juvenile literature.
4. Civil rights demonstrations—Washington (D.C.)—History—20th century—Juvenile literature.
5. African Americans—Biography—Juvenile literature. 6. Civil rights workers—
United States—Biography—Juvenile literature. I. Bates, Amy June, ill. II. Title.
E185.97.K5K84 2008
323.092—dc22
[B]
2008000987
ISBN-13: 978-1-4169-2774-7   ISBN-10: 1-4169-2774-3
0810 LAK

MARTIN'S DREAM

By Jane Kurtz

ILLUSTRATED BY
Amy June Bates

READY-TO-READ • ALADDIN
New York London Toronto Sydney

Martin Luther King
had a heart
so bold and strong.

He came one day
with things to say
to Washington, D.C.,
in 1963.

Two hundred thousand people
came together
on that day.

By bus, on skates,
from many states,
they came in like a stream,
looking for a dream.

They looked up at the face
of the man
who once declared,
in 1863,
all slaves must now be free.

But a law is just a start.
What can change a heart?

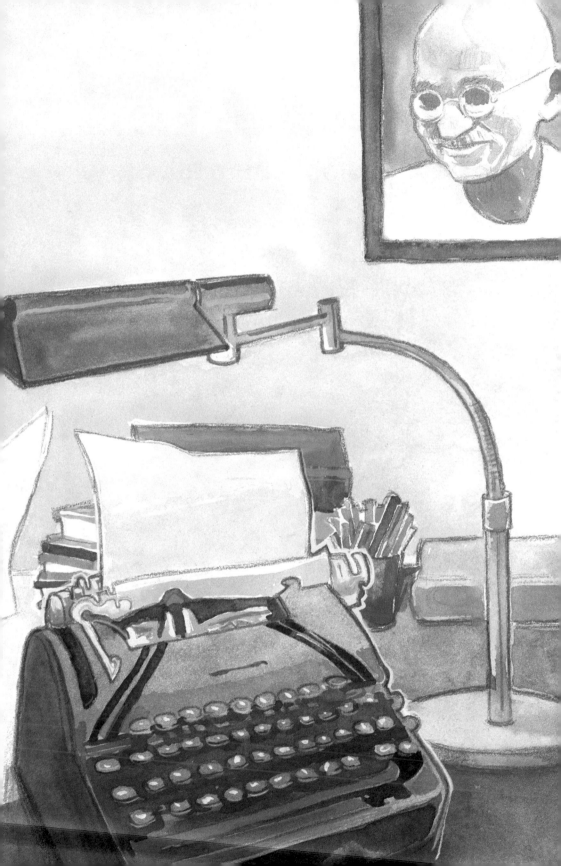

Martin Luther King
stood tall before them all.

He said
when it was time to vote
or play or work or ride,
no one should be outside.

The color of our skin
must not push us out or in.

Martin Luther King
almost sang
his words that day.

His voice rang out,
almost a shout.

When things are fair
everywhere,
then people will be free.
We will have liberty.

Martin Luther King
declared
that things can change.

Children can stand
hand in hand,
and we should all be able
to sit at the same table.

Martin Luther King
had a dream
so strong and clear,
some went away
changed that day.

His words were
bold and true.
His words
can change us too.

In all our hearts
let freedom ring
when we remember
Dr. King.